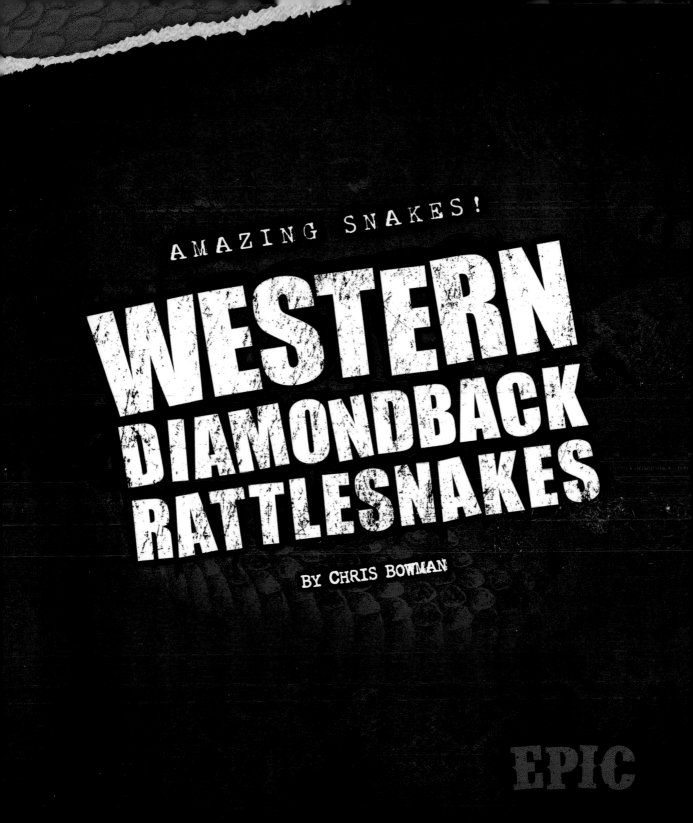

AMAZING SNAKES!

WESTERN DIAMONDBACK RATTLESNAKES

BY CHRIS BOWMAN

EPIC

BELLWETHER MEDIA • MINNEAPOLIS, MN

EPIC BOOKS are no ordinary books. They burst with intense action, high-speed heroics, and shadows of the unknown. Are you ready for an Epic adventure?

This edition first published in 2014 by Bellwether Media, Inc.

No part of this publication may be reproduced in whole or in part without written permission of the publisher. For information regarding permission, write to Bellwether Media, Inc., Attention: Permissions Department, 5357 Penn Avenue South, Minneapolis, MN 55419.

Library of Congress Cataloging-in-Publication Data

Bowman, Chris, 1990- author.
  Western Diamondback Rattlesnakes / by Chris Bowman.
    pages cm. – (Epic. Amazing Snakes!)
  Summary: "Engaging images accompany information about western diamondback rattlesnakes. The combination of high-interest subject matter and light text is intended for students in grades 2 through 7"– Provided by publisher.
  Audience: Ages 7-12.
  Audience: Grades 2 to 7.
  Includes bibliographical references and index.
  ISBN 978-1-62617-126-8 (hardcover : alk. paper)
  1. Western diamondback rattlesnake–Juvenile literature. I. Title.
  QL666.O69B68 2014
  597.96'38–dc23
                                                                    2013050083

Printed in the United States of America, North Mankato, MN.

TABLE OF CONTENTS

WHAT ARE WESTERN DIAMONDBACKS?

Western diamondbacks are known
for the rattle on the tip of their tail.
These rattlesnakes can grow up to
7 feet (2.1 meters) long.

The snakes have pink, red, brown, or gray scales. Dark diamonds cover their backs. Their tails have white and black bands.

WHERE WESTERN DIAMONDBACKS LIVE

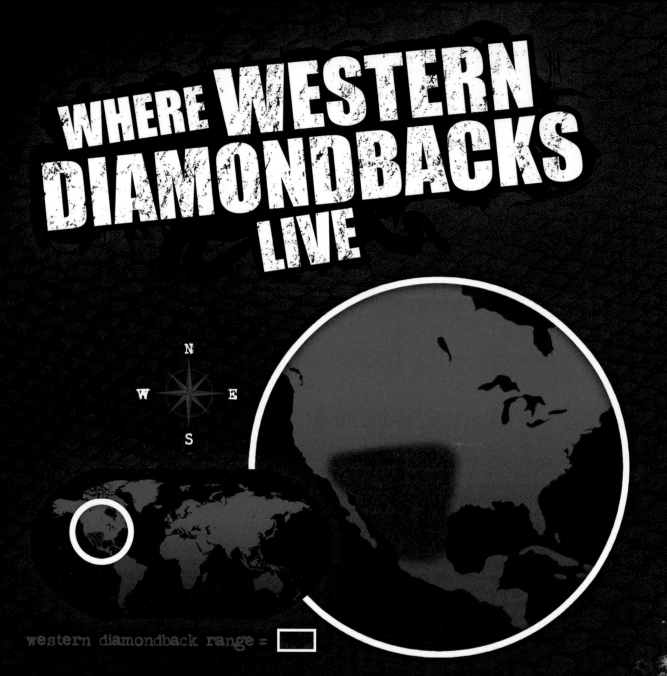

western diamondback range = ▭

Western diamondbacks are found in Mexico and the southwestern United States. They live in deserts, grasslands, and forests. They hibernate underground during the winter.

Out in the Cold

In the spring, the snakes are active during the day. They are more active at night during the hot summer.

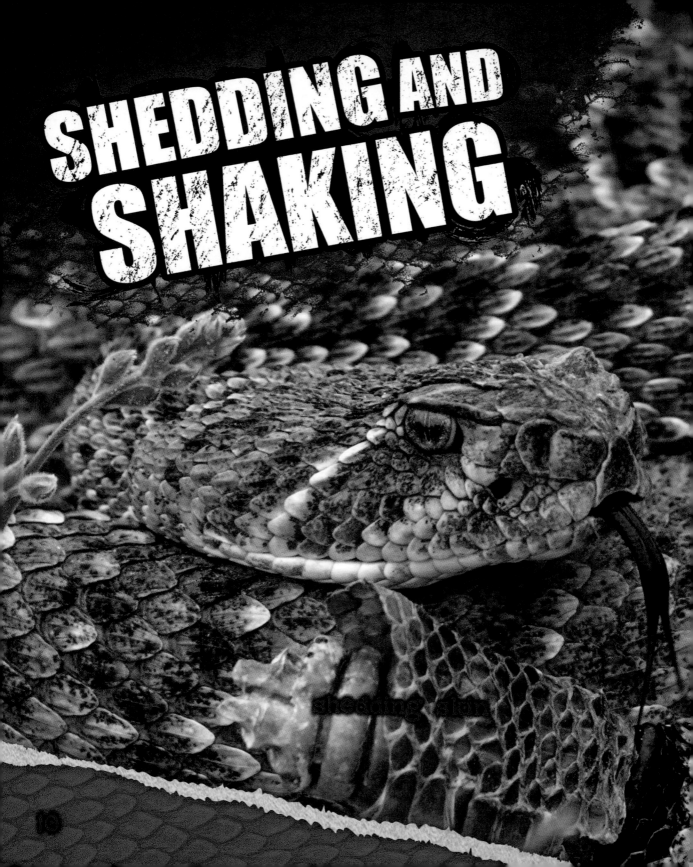

SHEDDING AND SHAKING

shedding a tail

Western diamondbacks shed their skin a few times a year. Only the last scale on the tail stays. This loose scale becomes a part of the rattle.

Can't See Straight

Their eyes get cloudy just before they shed their skin.

The snakes shake their rattle when they feel threatened. They have many predators. Roadrunners, coyotes, and raptors eat them. Cows and horses try to step on them.

Nervous Twitch

A western diamondback can shake its rattle more than 60 times per second.

HUNTING FOR PREY

Western diamondbacks ambush their prey. They lie still and wait for rats, birds, and rabbits to run past. They also use their pits to locate small animals nearby.

Western
Diamondback
Prey

Quiet as a Mouse

They sometimes put their body on top of their rattle. This helps them hunt quietly.

15

Loose Teeth

Sometimes the snakes lose their teeth in their prey. They can grow up to four pairs of fangs in a year.

A western diamondback strikes at prey with its fangs. These teeth inject strong venom into its catch. Then the rattlesnake lets the animal go. It will not get far.

The venom kills the animal quickly.
The western diamondback slithers
after its meal. Then it swallows its
catch whole!

No Rush

Diamondbacks usually eat every 2 to 3 weeks. However, they can live for two years without a meal!

SPECIES PROFILE

SCIENTIFIC NAME:	*CROTALUS ATROX*
NICKNAME:	COON-TAIL RATTLER
AVERAGE SIZE:	3-7 FEET (0.9-2.1 METERS)
HABITATS:	DESERTS, FORESTS, GRASSLANDS
COUNTRIES:	MEXICO, SOUTHWESTERN UNITED STATES
VENOMOUS:	YES
HUNTING METHOD:	AMBUSH, VENOMOUS BITE
COMMON PREY:	MICE, RATS, RABBITS GOPHERS, BIRDS, LIZARDS

GLOSSARY

ambush—to attack by surprise

fangs—sharp, hollow teeth; venom flows through fangs and into a bite.

hibernate—to spend the winter in a state of rest

inject—to force a liquid into something; venomous snakes inject venom into the bodies of prey.

pits—heat-sensing holes around the mouth; western diamondback rattlesnakes use pits to hunt for food at night.

predators—animals that hunt other animals for food

prey—animals that are hunted by other animals for food

raptors—birds of prey; raptors have excellent vision and sharp talons and beaks.

scales—small plates of skin that cover and protect a snake's body

shed—to lose a layer of skin; the layer that falls off is replaced by skin underneath it.

strikes—bites quickly and with force

threatened—in danger

venom—a poison created by a snake; snakes use venom to hurt or kill other animals.

TO LEARN MORE

At the Library

Leigh, Autumn. *Diamondback Rattlesnake*. New York, N.Y.: Gareth Stevens Pub., 2011.

Mattern, Joanne. *Rattlesnakes*. Mankato, Minn.: Capstone Press, 2009.

Raum, Elizabeth. *Rattlesnakes*. Mankato, Minn.: Amicus High Interest, 2014.

On the Web

Learning more about western diamondback rattlesnakes is as easy as 1, 2, 3.

1. Go to www.factsurfer.com.

2. Enter "western diamondback rattlesnakes" into the search box.

3. Click the "Surf" button and you will see a list of related web sites.

With factsurfer.com, finding more information is just a click away.

INDEX

The images in this book are reproduced through the courtesy of: Audrey Snider-Bell, front cover, pp. 16, 20-21; NaturePL / SuperStock, p. 5; Ryan M. Bolton, pp. 6-7; Cary Anderson/ Aurora Photos/ Alamy, p. 9; Animals Animals/ SuperStock, p. 10; Stephen McSweeny, p. 12; fivespots, p. 13; Bill Gorum/ Getty Images, pp. 14-15; Moments by Mullineux, p. 15 (top); Steve Byland, p. 15 (middle); J L Miller, p. 15 (bottom); DLILLC/ Corbis Images, p. 17; age fotostock/ SuperStock, pp. 18-19.